STEM
Waterworks

How Do CANALS Work?

First edition.

Christine Honders

PowerKiDS
press.

New York

Published in 2017 by The Rosen Publishing Group, Inc.
29 East 21st Street, New York, NY 10010

First Edition

Editor: Greg Roza
Book Design: Mickey Harmon

Photo Credits: Cover, pp. 1–32 (water) elic/Shutterstock.com; cover, pp. 1–32 (pipes) Kovalenko Alexander/Shutterstock.com; cover (image) Randy R/Shutterstock.com; p. 5 Ralf Gosch/Shutterstock.com; p. 7 lezumbalabernejena/Flickr.com; p. 9 Pecold/Shutterstock.com; p. 10 William H. Bond/National Geographic/Getty Images; p. 11 Kenneth Garrett/National Geographic/Getty Images; p. 13 J. L. Levy/Shutterstock.com; p. 15 https://commons.wikimedia.org/wiki/File:James_Brindley_by_Francis_Parsons.jpg; p. 17 phichet chaiyabin/Shutterstock.com; p. 19 https://upload.wikimedia.org/wikipedia/commons/6/6b/Montgomery_Canal_at_Redwith_Bridge_puddled.jpg; p. 21 https://en.wikipedia.org/wiki/File:Paddle_and_rymer_weir.jpg#/media/File:Paddle_and_rymer_weir.jpg; p. 22 Dmitry Naumov/Shutterstock.com; p. 23 A.B.G./Shutterstock.com; p. 25 https://commons.wikimedia.org/wiki/File:Inclined_Plane_9_West_near_port_Warren_from_HABS.png; p. 29 Simon Dannhauer/Shutterstock.com.

Library of Congress Cataloging-in-Publication Data

Names: Honders, Christine, author.
Title: How do canals work? / Christine Honders.
Description: New York : PowerKids Press, [2017] | Series: STEM waterworks | Includes index.
Identifiers: LCCN 2016011872 | ISBN 9781499419955 (pbk.) | ISBN 9781499419979 (library bound) | ISBN 9781499419962 (6 pack)
Subjects: LCSH: Canals–Juvenile literature. | Canals–History–Juvenile literature. | Canals, Interoceanic–Juvenile literature. | Waterways–Juvenile literature.
Classification: LCC TC745 .H66 2017 | DDC 386.4–dc23
LC record available at http://lccn.loc.gov/2016011872

Manufactured in the United States of America

CPSIA Compliance Information: Batch #BS16PK: For Further Information contact Rosen Publishing, New York, New York at 1-800-237-9932

Contents

Delivery by Boat

Have you ever received a package from someplace overseas? That package was put on a plane and flown to the United States, where it was taken by truck or train to your local post office and delivered to your door. Before airplanes, it wasn't that easy. Goods and packages were transported across the ocean by ship. Once the shipments arrived, how would they be delivered to the people who lived inland?

Canals solved that problem. Canals have been used by people for thousands of years. Not only do they make inland navigation easier and quicker, they're also used for **irrigation**, drainage, and even to generate electricity. This book shows how canals work and how STEM skills (science, technology, engineering, and math) are used to design and build them.

The Kiel Canal in Germany is the busiest canal in the world and connects the North and Baltic Seas. It's also capable of carrying much larger ships than most canals.

What Are Canals?

Canals are man-made waterways. They are used to transport goods, to drain low-lying lands, and to bring water to areas in need. Some canals are built to turn falling or fast-moving water into electricity. This is called hydroelectricity. Other canals are built to detour ships away from dangerous water conditions, such as rapids and waterfalls. The most important and most common use of canals today is for navigation.

Canals had the most impact on society during the 18th and 19th centuries. For **commodities** like coal or grains, which are shipped in large quantities, inland waterway transport is still the cheapest and most practical method of delivery. In the United States, almost 15 percent of freight delivered between states is carried by canals or navigable rivers.

Power canals are used to make electricity. The Queenston-Chippawa power canal in Niagara Falls, Canada, was completed in 1925 and at the time was part of the largest hydroelectric project in the world.

In the Pipe

Navigable rivers are deep and wide enough for water travel. Rivers can be made navigable by making them deeper or straighter, which is called canalization. The U.S. inland waterway system has 12,000 miles (19,312 km) of navigable waterways!

Early Canals

The earliest canals were made for irrigation and to create navigable waterways. In the seventh century BC, the Assyrians built a 50-mile (80.5 km) canal to bring freshwater into the city of Nineveh. Other records describe Babylonian King Nebuchadnezzar II's (c. 630–c. 561 BC) royal canal, which connected the Tigris and Euphrates Rivers. The ancient Sumerians, Phoenicians, Persians, Egyptians, and Romans, constructed canal systems.

The oldest canal that's still used today is the Grand Canal in China. It may have been started as early as the fourth century BC and was used to transport troops and tax collectors. It was finished in AD 1280 and is a grand total of 1,114 miles (1,793 km) long. It's still the longest navigable canal in the world.

In the Pipe

Engineer Pierre-Paul Riquet (1609–1680) built the Canal du Midi in southern France. It was a massive project, but Riquet's engineering and problem-solving skills made it an inspiration for other large canal projects, particularly the Panama and Suez Canals.

Riquet's Canal du Midi includes bridges and tunnels that are structural marvels. This **aqueduct** was built to carry boats over the Orb River, and it's still used today.

The Industrial Revolution (c. 1760–1850) was a time in Europe and America when new technologies emerged. Inventions like the steam engine led to increased production in new factories. More waterways were needed to transport larger and heavier goods more quickly. This led to the beginning of the "canal era," especially in England and America.

George Washington knew that canals were important to the growth of the United States. In 1785, he was named the first president of the Patowmack Canal Company, which created the Patowmack Canal along the Potomac River.

Shown here is a part of the Patowmack Canal that is still standing.

Canals had a major impact on expansion into the American West. Farmers were settling further west and needed a way to send their crops to large coastal cities like New York or Philadelphia. They also needed manufactured goods for their farms. Transporting goods by wagon was costly and time consuming. Canals allowed farmers on the frontier to get supplies more easily and cheaply. They also allowed farmers to send their crops to eastern cities, and then to Europe.

The Erie Canal

In 1817, a project was started to connect the Hudson River to Lake Erie. The Erie Canal was a technological marvel with 83 locks. Eighteen aqueducts carried canal boats over other bodies of water. The Niagara **Escarpment** proved to be a major challenge to builders. In Lockport, New York, workers built five levels of locks with two lanes that climbed about 80 feet (24 m) in order to overcome the escarpment.

The canal was finished on October 26, 1825, and was an instant success. The cost of bringing goods from Buffalo to New York City went from $100 per ton to $10 per ton. Trade increased dramatically, causing traffic jams on the canal and making it necessary to widen it so that more boats could travel in each direction.

Although railroads, highways, and airplanes eventually made the Erie Canal **obsolete**, it helped the United States to grow into a wealthy, powerful nation.

In the Pipe

Almost no trained engineers were involved in building the Erie Canal because there were no engineering schools in the United States at the time. It became a training ground for would-be engineers. They then took their knowledge to the rest of the country.

Engineering a Canal

It takes specialized engineering knowledge to design and create canals and related structures. Canal travel has more **restrictions** than other methods of transportation. Highways and railroads are more adaptable to the natural landscape and are more easily designed to go over mountains and rivers, while waterways are typically restricted to flatter ground. Modern canal engineers want their projects to stay competitive with the railroad system, so they have to design canals to carry large shipments as quickly as possible to keep costs down.

While planning a canal, engineers need to consider changes in elevation. They must plan the best ways of reaching water sources and keeping water in the canal. Building canals doesn't just depend on engineering skills; knowledge of science, technology, and math is a must!

James Brindley (1716–1772) was one of the world's first canal engineers. Born in England, he was involved with about 360 canal projects. His work set the standard for most future canal designs.

Designing and Digging

Before digging, scientists and engineers use math and geometry to determine how big the canal should be. Canals are usually cut in a trapezoidal shape, with a flat base, or "bed," and sides that slope outward. The bed must be three to four times as wide as the largest vessels traveling on the canal, and the surface has to be six to eight times as wide. This shape allows the water to flow more smoothly. Engineers use mathematical formulas to determine the best width for a canal.

Canals were dug by hand until 1665, when gunpowder was used in France. Today, modern machines such as cranes and excavators remove the dirt and pile it on each side of the canal, making berms. Scrapers and dump trucks easily travel over rough terrain and get rid of excess dirt.

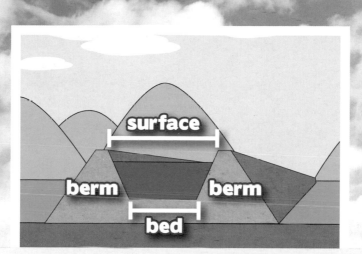

surface

berm

berm

bed

The trapezoidal design allows the most water to move freely on all sides of the ship. If a ship takes up too much space in a canal, waves make it more difficult to move the ship.

In the Pipe

Berms are raised banks on either side of a canal. Before steam engines became common, flattened berms were used as towpaths, where animals or a group of men would walk while towing the ships by rope.

After the canal has been dug, science is used to determine how well it will hold water. Water seeps into dirt and rocks, and certain rocks are more porous than others. That means liquids filter more easily through them. Geologists, or scientists who study Earth and what it's made of, study the rocks in the walls and floor of the canal to see how porous they are.

In the 18th century, the most popular method of waterproofing canals was "puddling." Puddle is a mixture of sand, clay, and water that's spread on the inside of a canal. When it dries, this mixture becomes waterproof. As concrete, plastic sheeting, and asphalt have become available, they are often used instead. **Embankments** also have to be waterproofed to protect them from washing away.

Puddling is still used today. Shown here, puddle clay is used to restore parts of the Montgomery Canal in England, which was originally constructed in the late 1800s.

In the Pipe

Scientists who study water and its qualities are called hydrologists. They determine whether there's enough water nearby to keep a canal filled. Ecologists study the effects a canal will have on the local environment.

Locks

Some of the biggest difficulties engineers face when building canals are changes in the elevation of the land. Locks are water **basins** used for raising and lowering boats between different levels. Most have a rectangular shape.

The oldest lock design was the flash lock, which was used by the Egyptians and Chinese as early as the third century BC. Flash locks had a gate on one end that, when opened, let out a rush of water that would carry the boat downstream. This was dangerous because it used large amounts of water and the speed of the water couldn't be controlled. If a boat needed to go upstream, people or animals dragged it through the gate by rope.

This flash lock was made of paddles attached to a horizontal board. The paddles could be removed, letting a "flash" of water rush downstream.

Locks were improved in AD 984 when the first pound lock was used on China's Grand Canal. Its design included two gates at both ends of the basin, allowing water to be **impounded** between them. Pound locks raise and lower ships by trapping and releasing water.

A boat traveling upstream enters the lock at the lower level. Once it's in the lock the lower gates close and water is pumped into the basin. The water rises, lifting the boat to the high water level. Then the upper gate is opened and the boat goes through.

Several locks may be needed to lift a vessel over uneven land. The locks of the Panama Canal lift ships over sea level near one end of the canal and lower them back down on the other side.

In the Pipe

In the 1480s, Italian engineer and artist Leonardo da Vinci created the miter gate lock. Miter gates swing on hinges and meet in a V-shape, pointing upstream so the water pressure seals them shut. Miter gates are still commonly used in canals today.

miter gate

Many canals need more than one lock to raise or lower a ship to the right level. You can think of locks as stairways for ships!

The Growth of Canal Technology

New technology made canals simpler and safer. At one time, water pouring into a basin from an opening upper gate caused rough waters that could damage ships. Starting in the 17th century, **valve**-controlled openings were added to basins, resulting in smoother, safer passage. Lock gates once made of wood are now made of much stronger materials, such as steel-reinforced concrete. Electrical and **hydraulic** power are now used to open gates.

In the 1800s, the Morris Canal in New Jersey made a huge leap in canal technology by using inclined planes to move ships out of the canal, over hills, and back into the canal. At the bottom of the slope, a ship entered a cradle that was attached to a cable. Water-powered **turbines** were used to pull the cradles up the slope and then lower them down the other side.

The Morris Canal had 1,674 feet (510 m) of elevation change, which is more than any other canal in the world. Its 23 inclined planes moved boats faster and used less water than locks.

In the Pipe

The Houston Ship Channel started as a shallow waterway connecting the Gulf of Mexico to Houston. Starting in 1910, the channel was made deeper and wider to accommodate large ships, turning landlocked Houston into one of the busiest port cities in the world!

Canals That Connect Seas

The Suez Canal crosses the Isthmus of Suez in Egypt and provides a sea route between the Mediterranean and Red Seas. In 1859, a French diplomat named Ferdinand de Lesseps began construction on the canal. It took 10 years to complete and is 101 miles (162.5 km) long. It forever changed the trading industry by letting ships avoid the dangerous trip around Africa.

In 1881, de Lesseps started work on the Panama Canal, which would connect the Atlantic and Pacific Oceans. He was unsuccessful in completing the canal due to construction problems and yellow fever in the region. It was completed by U.S. engineer John F. Stevens in 1914. The canal, at 41 miles (66 km) long, lifts vessels up through three stepped locks to Gatun Lake, and down three locks on the other side.

The Panama Canal crosses the tiny Central American country of Panama. It revolutionized world trading by sea and is one of the greatest engineering accomplishments ever achieved.

Gatun Lake

Atlantic Ocean

Pacific Ocean

locks

locks

In the Pipe

Construction on the Suez Canal started with forced labor using picks and shovels. In 1863, forced labor was banned and coal-powered shovels and dredges were used to dig the remaining 75 percent of the canal.

The End of the Canal Era

Canals have their share of problems. Travel is often slow, especially compared to planes and trains. In cold places, frozen water makes canal travel impossible. Droughts affect water levels, and severe weather and flooding can wash away embankments. The biggest downfall of canals during their height was the railroad system, which was a much cheaper and faster way to transport goods. However, canals are still used today to transport bulk goods and for recreation.

In 2014, construction was started on a canal across the Central American country of Nicaragua, creating a second route between the Atlantic and the Pacific. The Nicaraguan government believes the canal will create jobs and bring people out of poverty within the next five years. However, some scientists believe this canal will be an environmental disaster.

In the Pipe

Biologists are concerned that the proposed canal route will harm Lake Nicaragua and **contaminate** the water with bacteria, killing natural wildlife. Other worries include the possible damming of the San Juan River, which could dry up other rivers and cause water shortages.

Lake Nicaragua, which is six times the size of Los Angeles, is a major source of drinking water and irrigation. Digging in it could be devastating to the local people.

Opening Gates to New Worlds

Canals have played an important role in the history of the United States, as well as other countries around the world. The Panama and Suez Canals connected seas, creating quicker and safer travel routes that expanded trade between countries around the world. The Erie Canal brought industry and commerce to the Midwest and made shipping crops and supplies much easier and cheaper. It also helped cities like Buffalo and New York City grow and prosper.

As science and technology continue to improve, canal engineers and builders are sure to come up with new **innovations** to make canal travel even easier and quicker. With the skill, knowledge, and technology we have today, who knows what path canals will lead us down next?

Glossary

aqueduct: A pathway constructed to guide water from a source into a populated area.

basin: A container for holding liquid.

commodity: A raw material or product that can be bought and sold.

contaminate: Pollute.

embankment: A wall of earth or stone built to stop a river from flooding an area.

escarpment: A long, steep slope separating areas of land that are different heights.

hydraulic: Operated using the pressure of a liquid.

impound: To collect and store water in a reservoir or other location.

innovation: A new invention, or a new way of doing things.

irrigation: The watering of a dry area by man-made means in order to grow plants.

obsolete: Outdated and no longer in use.

restriction: Something that limits or controls.

turbine: A motor operated by the movement of water, steam, or air.

valve: Something that controls the movement of liquids or gases through tubes or vessels.

Index

Websites

Due to the changing nature of Internet links, PowerKids Press has developed an online list of websites related to the subject of this book. This site is updated regularly. Please use this link to access the list: www.powerkidslinks.com/sww/canal